AUSTRALIA

VISIONS OF A CONTINENT

NEW
HOLLAND

Published in Australia by
New Holland Publishers (Australia) Pty Ltd
Sydney • Auckland • London • Cape Town
14 Aquatic Drive Frenchs Forest NSW 2086 Australia
218 Lake Road Northcote Auckland New Zealand
86 Edgware Road London W2 2EA United Kingdom
80 McKenzie Street Cape Town 8001 South Africa

First published in 1998

Photographic credits
All photographs © **Shaen Adey/NHIL**
with the exception of the following:
Vicki Hastrich/NHIL: p87 (bottom); **Anthony
Johnson/NHIL**: pp33, 35, 60, 94, 96, 120, 122–123,
124; **Jiri Lochman/Lochman Transparencies**: p90;
NHIL: pp47, 48, 69 (left); courtesy of **Phillip Island
Penguin Reserve**: p42 (bottom); **Nick Rains/NHIL**:
pp16–17, 20 (bottom), 24.

National Library of Australia
    Cataloguing-in-Publication Data:

Australia: visions of a continent

ISBN(10) 1 86436 371 1
ISBN(13) 978-1-86436-371-5

1. Australia – Pictorial works

919.40222

10 9 8 7 6 5

Half-title page: Colourful bathing huts on Brighton
    Beach, south of Melbourne
Title page: The Sydney Opera House at sunset.
This page: Roads stretch endlessly across the vast
    outback of the Australian continent.

CONTENTS

AUSTRALIA

VISIONS OF A CONTINENT

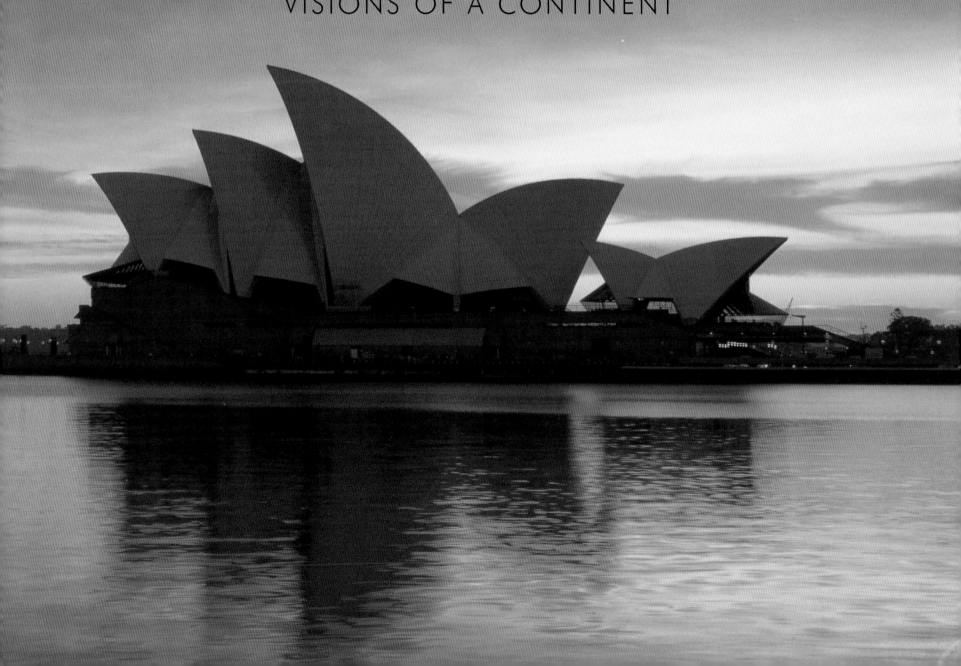

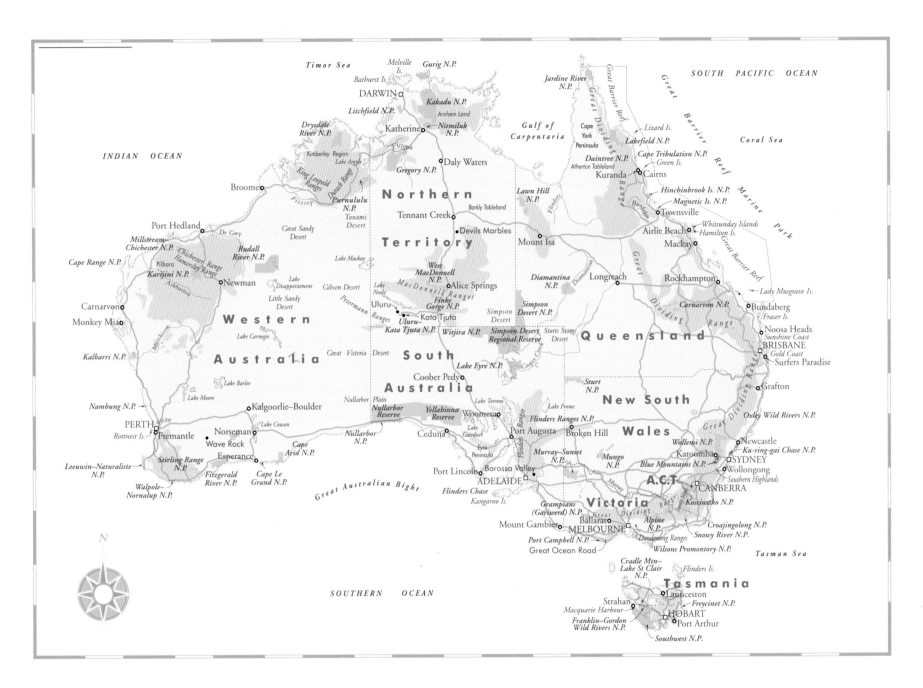

Above: The Australian continent stretches for over 3600 kilometres from north to south and for over 4000 kilometres from east to west.

INTRODUCTION

Covering an area of over 7,500,000 square kilometres, the vast island continent of Australia encompasses unique flora and fauna, cosmopolitan cities and a wealth of scenic splendour. Divided into six states and two territories, it is a country with something for everyone, from the lush, primeval rainforest of the Daintree to the harsh, unrelenting deserts of the outback, from the underwater kaleidoscope of the Great Barrier Reef — the world's largest coral structure — to the haunting beauty of Uluru — the world's largest monolith.

This rich diversity is continued in the population. First inhabited by Aboriginal people and then settled as a penal colony by the British, Australia today is home to an eclectic mix of cultures, with recent Asian immigration having swelled the ranks of the earlier European arrivals. Cities such as Sydney and Melbourne with their Chinatowns, Thai restaurants, and Greek

Wildflowers carpet the West Australian landscape.

and Italian quarters vividly reflect the changing face of modern Australia and, with nearly 90 per cent of the population living in the urban areas of the eastern, southern and south-western coasts, it is a face with which most Australians are increasingly familiar.

But it is the land and its wildlife for which the country is best known. Australia is one of the oldest continents and has remained free of major geological activity for the past 80 million years. As a result of this stability and the continent's geographical isolation, a strange and often unique fauna was able to develop in relative safety, giving rise to, among others, the koalas and kangaroos that have come to symbolise Australia for the international visitor. The floral kingdom is no less spectacular — the several thousand species of wildflower that blossom after the rains in Western Australia form one of the richest plant communities in the world.

For the traveller to Australia, there is much to see and do. New South Wales proclaims itself the Premier State and as its capital Sydney — home to both the Opera House and Harbour Bridge — prepares to host the 2000 Olympics, it is certainly at the forefront of Australian endeavour. The federal capital, Canberra, nestles in the Australian Captial Territory, while further south lie the green fields of Victoria, the tree-lined boulevards of Melbourne, and the breathtaking vistas and tortured rock formations of the Great Ocean Road. South Australia is the state of arts and culture. The biennial Adelaide Festival is a celebration of drama, music, literature and dance, while the Barossa Valley produces wines of international standing. Smallest of the states, Tasmania is known for its historic sites and forested wilderness — an adventure lover's paradise! In stark contrast is Western Australia, occupying one-third of Australia's landmass. Much of the land is arid and inhospitable, dotted with mysterious formations such as the limestone Pinnacles of Nambung National Park and offering a wealth of dramatic scenery. Visitors can also explore the wonders of the Northern Territory — the wetlands of Kakadu National Park, the frontier town of Alice Springs, and the glowing rocks of Uluru and Kata Tjuta. And finally, Queensland invites one to relax and enjoy the 'sunshine' lifestyle of sand, surf and glorious tropical islands.

Above: Internationally famed icons of Sydney — the breathtaking Opera House and Harbour Bridge.

Above: Fireworks light up the harbour in a spectacular New Year's Eve display.

Right: Australia's oldest and largest city, Sydney is a sprawling metropolis
of nearly four million people.

These pages: Every year on 26 January, the country celebrates Australia Day, commemorating the arrival of the First Fleet. The harbour is the focal point of Sydney's festivities with crowds gathering to watch the various boat races.

Above: Sydney's Town Hall, with its ornately decorated façade, is a fine example of Victorian architecture.

Above: Once Sydney's produce market, the beautifully restored Queen Victoria Building is now an upmarket shopping centre.

These pages: The annual Sydney Gay and Lesbian Mardi Gras is one of the city's major tourist attractions, with over three-quarters of a million spectators all jostling to catch a glimpse of the flamboyant participants.

Previous pages: Seen from the west, Anzac Bridge dominates the city skyline. To the right, the giant cotton reel of Sydney Tower reaches more than 300 metres into the sky.

These pages: Bondi Beach is Australia's most famous stretch of sand. Whether surfing or simply strolling along the shore and cafe-lined esplanade, Bondi's appeal is inescapable.

Above: Palm Beach, the most exclusive of Sydney's northern beaches, offers superb vistas out towards Barrenjoey Head.

These pages: Vines were established in the Hunter Valley in 1858 and it has become one of Australia's best known wine-producing areas. Many of the vineyards offer cellar tastings.

Above: Situated on the far north coast, Byron Bay is one of New South Wales' most well-known holiday destinations. The lighthouse at Cape Byron marks the most easterly point of the Australian mainland.

Left: The coastal town of Port Macquarie lies north of Sydney and is a popular tourist and fishing location.

Above: The Three Sisters are one of the most famous formations in the Blue Mountains, situated to the west of Sydney.

Right: The blue haze which gives the mountains their name is supposedly created by light filtering through the vapour given off by the eucalypt forests.

Above: The lush green fields around Berry, on the New South Wales South Coast, are at the centre of the state's dairy farming region.

Above: Perisher Valley in Kosciuszko National Park is one of Australia's most popular skiing destinations.

Above: Commonwealth Park is just one of the many gardens for which Canberra, Australia's capital, is famed.

Top: Canberra is a city of modern architecture. This sculpture of a cyclist stands in front of the National Science and Technology Centre.

Right: The unique grass-topped New Parliament House on Capital Hill looks out over Lake Burley Griffin towards the National War Memorial.

Above: Stained-glass windows in the National War Memorial commemorate those service personnel who gave their lives for Australia.

Left: The War Memorial is both a museum and shrine. Opened in 1941, it was designed to resemble a Byzantine church.

Previous pages: Melbourne, state capital of Victoria, lies on the shores of Port Phillip Bay.

Above: The Victorian Arts Centre is the cultural heart of Melbourne and comprises several theatre venues, a concert hall, a performing arts museum, and the National Gallery of Victoria.

Right: From the south bank of the Yarra River, one can look across to the city's business heart.

Above: Trams are a popular means of public transport throughout the city of Melbourne.

Left and top: Brunswick Street in the suburb of Fitzroy is lined with colourful shops, cafes and pubs.

Above and top: The Little Penguins of Phillip Island come ashore every night under cover of darkness to return to their rookeries. A visitors centre caters to the large number of tourists who come to watch this penguin 'parade'.

Right: The town of Cowes on Phillip Island attracts holidaymakers to its beach and pier.

Previous pages and left: Victoria's rugged coastline boasts dramatic formations such as the Twelve Apostles — stone pillars that have been eroded over the centuries into tortured forms.

Above: The Loch Ard Gorge takes its name from a shipwreck that occurred there in 1878. Tragically, only two of the 50 souls on board survived.

Above: Puffing Billy is a popular attraction for visitors to the Dandenong Ranges. The restored steam
train travels from Belgrave to Emerald Lake each day.

Right: The farmlands of the Yarra Valley form a striking contrast to the lush forest that covers the nearby Dandenongs.

Above: MacKenzie Falls are one of four waterfalls formed as the MacKenzie River plunges over the Great Dividing Range's escarpment.

Above: The Grampians (Gariwerd) National Park encompasses a region of rugged sandstone peaks, rocky overhangs and rich forests.

Above: Displaying life as it was during the time of the early settlers, Tyntyndyer Homestead near Swan Hill is now a National Trust building.

Top: Grapes are put out to dry in Mildura, far north-west Victoria. The raisins produced in the region are an important Australian export.

Left: Sovereign Hill, near Ballarat, is a recreation of a 19th-century goldrush town.

Above: With a population of around 200 000, Hobart, capital of Tasmania, has managed to retain a strong sense of community.

Right: Mount Wellington offers a perfect vantage point to view the city, the Tasman Bridge and the picturesque Derwent River Valley.

Previous pages: Sleepy Victoria Dock is home to Hobart's fishing fleet. However, during the annual Sydney-Hobart Yacht Race it becomes a hive of activity.

Above: The houses of Arthurs Circus in historic Battery Point were built by convicts for the more well-to-do residents of early Hobart.

Left: Every weekend, visitors and locals flock to the markets held among the carefully restored Georgian buildings of Salamanca Place.

Above: The ruins of the penal settlement at Port Arthur, which date from the 1800s, are now being painstakingly preserved. They are a powerful reminder of the country's convict past.

Opposite: The Devils Kitchen is just one of several dramatic rock formations on the Tasman Peninsula.

Above: Red-necked Wallabies are a common sight in the open woodland areas of Tasmania.

Left: Crater Lake in Cradle Mountain–Lake St Clair National Park is one of the highlights of the demanding 85-kilometre Overland Walking Track.

Following pages: Tasmania, with its many unpolluted lakes, is widely believed to offer some of the best wild trout fishing in the world.

Above: Hindley Street is the hub of Adelaide's nightlife with a selection of nightclubs, restaurants and cafes to suit all tastes.

Above: South Australia's graceful state capital is set on the banks of the tranquil River Torrens.

Above left: The clearly visible spires of St Peter's Cathedral make it easy to understand why Adelaide is known as the 'City of Churches'.

Above right: The Adelaide Festival Centre is one of the venues for the city's biennial Arts Festival which attracts both local and international performers.

Left: Adelaide's only tram runs from the city centre to the popular beachside suburb of Glenelg.

Above: The Barossa Valley was originally settled by German immigrants. The architecture of Chateau Yaldara displays this influence.

Right: Much of Australia's top wine is produced by the vineyards of the Barossa Valley.

Previous pages: The treacherous coastline of Kangaroo Island has claimed many a ship.

Above left: Caves, sinkholes and limestone rock formations are a feature of the island —
all created by the erosive power of the elements.

Above right: Paul's Place wildlife farm allows visitors to see native fauna being rehabilitated.

Left: Approximately 500 sea lions make their home at the island's Seal Bay. Accustomed to the
presence of humans, these animals are protected by the conservation park.

Above: The opal fields around Coober Pedy are pitted with abandoned prospecting holes.

Top: To escape the heat, some residents of Coober Pedy have built their homes underground.

Right: From above, there is little to hint at the activity that goes on below ground.

Above: The Burswood Island Resort and Casino is situated just outside the centre of Perth on the banks of the Swan River.

Left: Skyscrapers dominate the Perth skyline — evidence of the economic boom that took place during the 1980s.

Above: With a perfect climate and easy access to the river and sea, it is hardly suprising that one in four Perth residents owns a boat.

Above: Built by convicts as a gaol, Fremantle's Round House is now the state's oldest surviving building.

Previous pages: The gracious Customs House in Fremantle dates from colonial times.

Above: Rottnest Island is home to large colonies of quokkas, a small species of marsupial.

Top and right: Only 19 kilometres from Perth, tranquil Rottnest Island with its unspoilt bays and crystal-clear water is a popular weekend getaway.

Above: Wave Rock near Hyden is a granite 'breaker' that has been sculpted by wind erosion.

Top: Driving across the Nullarbor, the unwary motorist can encounter several unusual hazards!

Left: The road stretches in an unwavering line for miles across the featureless Nullarbor Plain.

Following pages: Limestone pillars known as the Pinnacles rise out of the desert in Nambung National Park, casting eerie shadows across the sand.

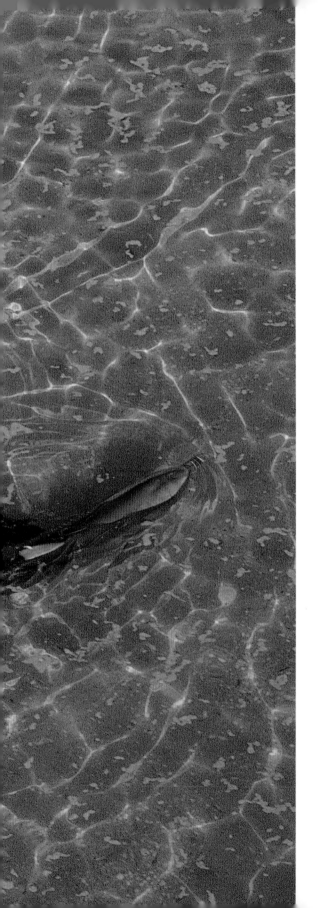

Above: The stromatolites of Hamelin Pool date back some 3500 million years, making them the world's second-oldest known fossil. Hamelin Pool forms part of the Shark Bay Marine Park.

Left: At Monkey Mia in Shark Bay, a thriving tourism industry has developed around the dolphins that swim to shore each day to be hand fed.

Above: Just outside Port Hedland, vast expanses of glistening salt wait to be shipped overseas.

Right: Once the pearling capital of the world, tourism is now increasingly important to Broome, with camel rides being offered along Cable Beach.

Above: A tropical sunset over Darwin's Fannie Bay is an experience not to be missed!

Left: Bombed during World War II and destroyed by Cyclone Tracy in 1974, Darwin has recovered to become a flourishing modern city.

Above: Darwin's strong Asian influence is evident at the Mindil Beach markets where people come to shop as the sun sets.

Above: The life of a 'jackeroo' on the vast Northern Territory cattle stations has changed little over the years.

Above left, and right: Nourlangie Rock in Kakadu National Park is an important Aboriginal rock-art site. Here, the 'Lightning Man' holds his arc of light.

Above right: From the lookout at Ubirr, the visitor can obtain sweeping views of Kakadu's wetlands which abound with animal and plantlife as soon as the first rains arrive.

Above: During the wet season, huge numbers of migratory waterbirds — including the black-necked stork, or jabiru — flock to Kakadu.

Left: A cruise on Yellow Waters enables visitors to observe the region's birdlife as well as its fearsome saltwater crocodiles.

Above and right: The rocky outcrops known as the Devils Marbles, near Tennant Creek, are — according to Aboriginal legend — the eggs of the Rainbow Serpent.

Top: South of Darwin lies Katherine Gorge which, over the millennia, has been carved out of the sandstone rock by the Katherine River.

Above: Alice Springs started life as an overland telegraph station, but is now a modern town with a population of over 20 000.

Above: The majestic cliffs of Rainbow Valley are streaked with bands of colour, making them particularly impressive at sunrise and sunset.

Previous pages: The world's largest monolith, Uluru (formerly known as Ayers Rock) rises an imposing 348 metres above the surrounding landscape.

These pages: Kata Tjuta means 'many heads' in the local Aboriginal language — an accurate description of this famous formation's numerous domes.

Above: Modern glass buildings such as the Brisbane Conference and Exhibition Centre contrast with the city's remaining Victorian and Edwardian buildings.

Left: Capital of Queensland, Brisbane is built on the banks of the meandering Brisbane River, just a few kilometres inland from Moreton Bay.

Above: An artificial beach has been created at South Bank, the site of Expo '88 and located only a few minutes from the city centre.

Above: Pleasure boats and barges buzz constantly up and down the Brisbane River against a backdrop of soaring skyscrapers.

These pages: Surfers Paradise is the glittering heart of Queensland's Gold Coast. High-rise buildings crowd the shoreline while locals and tourists flock to the beach to enjoy lazy days of summer sun.

Following pages: Surfing is a way of life on the Gold Coast and as the sun creeps over the horizon, the first enthusiasts head off in search of the perfect wave.

Above: The sparkling waters of the Great Barrier Reef invite snorkellers and divers to explore a wonderland of marine treasures.

Right: Heron Island, an important marine biology research site, is known for the diversity of its reef life as well as for the green turtles which come ashore every year to lay their eggs.

Above: Tjapukai Aboriginal Cultural Park introduces visitors to traditional Aboriginal life.

Top: A scenic railway runs between Cairns and the town of Kuranda on the Atherton Tablelands.

Left: The tropical town of Cairns is the departure point for many trips to the Great Barrier Reef.

These pages: The Great Barrier Reef covers more than 230 000 square kilometres and is a complex ecosystem of tiny sand cays, palm-fringed islands and over 2000 separate reefs.

These pages: To the north of Cairns lies the World Heritage area of Daintree National Park. Its lush tropical rainforest extends down to the ocean in places and provides a habitat for a rich diversity of flora and fauna, many species of which are unique to the region.

These pages and following page: Cape York, the northernmost point of Queensland, has largely remained a region of untamed wilderness where desolate beaches and seemingly impenetrable mangrove forest recall a time before European settlement.